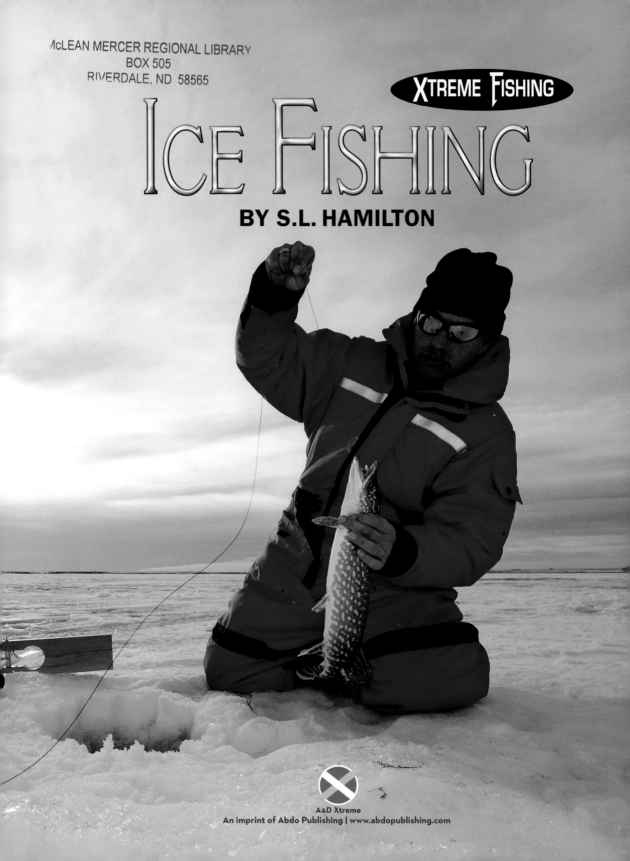

XTREME FISHING

ICE FISHING

BY S.L. HAMILTON

A&D Xtreme
An imprint of Abdo Publishing | www.abdopublishing.com

Visit us at
www.abdopublishing.com

Published by Abdo Publishing Company, a division of ABDO, PO Box 398166, Minneapolis, Minnesota 55439. Copyright ©2015 by Abdo Consulting Group, Inc. International copyrights reserved in all countries. No part of this book may be reproduced in any form without written permission from the publisher. A&D Xtreme™ is a trademark and logo of Abdo Publishing Company.

Printed in the United States of America, North Mankato, Minnesota.
102014
012015

 PRINTED ON RECYCLED PAPER

Editor: John Hamilton
Graphic Design: Sue Hamilton
Cover Design: Sue Hamilton
Cover Photo: Alamy
Interior Photos: Angel-GUARD Products-pg 29 (inset); Annual Lake Minnetonka Crappie Flop Ice Fishing Tournament-pg 14 (inset); AP-pgs 8-9, 10, 16-17 & 28-29; Corbis-pgs 12-13; Dreamstime-pgs 2-3, 6, 7 & 14-15; Eskimo-pg 6 (inset); Don Lepper-pgs 22-23; Glow Images-pg 11; iStock-pgs 1, 17 (inset), 30-31 & 32; James Smedley-pgs 4-5, 18-19, 20-21, 24-25 & 26-27.

Websites
To learn more about Fishing, visit booklinks.abdopublishing.com. These links are routinely monitored and updated to provide the most current information available.

Library of Congress Control Number: 2014944877

Cataloging-in-Publication Data

Hamilton, S.L.
 Ice fishing / S.L. Hamilton.
   p. cm. -- (Xtreme fishing)
ISBN 978-1-62403-682-8 (lib. bdg.)
Includes index.
1. Ice fishing--Juvenile literature.   I. Title.
799.12/2--dc23

                              2014944877

Contents

Ice Fishing

Fishermen bore holes in the ice and drop their lines into the watery depths. Are fish there? It takes time and patience to discover the best ice fishing spots.

Ice fishermen dress for the cold. Some fish in the open air, sitting on a folding seat or bucket. Many others set up ice houses for protection and comfort. They are prepared to take on both freezing weather and finicky fish. Ice fishing is a fun wintertime sport for those unafraid of the cold.

XTREME QUOTE – *"The more you know about a winter lake, the more fish will be piled up in front of you."* –Jim Capossela, author and ice fisherman

Drilling Holes

To fish in the winter, anglers use chisels or augers to bore holes in the ice. Ice chisels and hand augers make less noise and are lighter to carry than motorized augers.

Some ice chisels come apart, which makes carrying them easier.

Hand Auger

If ice is thicker than 12 inches (30 cm), or the fisherman needs to drill a number of holes, an electric- or gas-powered auger is a fast, convenient device. However, powered augers are heavy. Since anglers have to carry all their gear onto the ice, convenience must be balanced against weight.

Powered Auger

XTREME FACT – Loud chopping or drilling can scare away game fish. Ice fishermen try to be as quiet as possible when drilling their holes and when walking on ice.

Ice Houses

Ice houses give fishermen protection from the cold and an added level of comfort. Some are simple tents or wooden "shacks," while others have all the conveniences of home, including beds, televisions, stoves, and portable toilets. Specially designed heaters are brought to some ice houses as well.

This ice house in Meredith, New Hampshire, is known as "The Lodge." It contains luxuries such as a television and stove.

XTREME FACT – An ice house may also be called a fish shanty, fish shack, fish hut, or bob house.

9

Tip-Ups & Ice Rods

A tip-up is a fishing rig with a spool of line attached to the bottom. It sends up a flag to alert the angler when a fish is on the line. An angler may also use a jiggle stick or jig rod. These poles are wiggled back and forth or jerked up and down to tempt the fish to bite. They are 2 to 3 feet (.6 to .9 m) in length.

XTREME QUOTE – *"Remember that fish that are under the ice aren't willing to expend a lot of energy to catch their food... The best thing to do is find the depth where the fish are. Then drop your bait or lure right in front of the fish so it's easy for them to bite it."* —Drew Cushing, angler & wildlife biologist

Ice rods are short and extremely lightweight. They are specifically designed for ice fishing. The reel is usually attached to the pole using electrical tape instead of cold metal or plastic rings that typically hold a reel to a rod. Tape is warmer and holds better in freezing weather.

Yellow Perch

Yellow perch are active winter fish, but they are roamers. They may be found in shallow, weedy areas or in deeper, weedless flat lake bottoms.

Yellow perch are smaller-sized fish and good eating. They range in length from 7 to 15 inches (18 to 38 cm). Since perch of similar sizes often school together, ice fishermen who end up catching perch that are too small will move to another hole. Yellow perch are daytime feeders. They bite on small minnows or 1- to 2-inch (2.5- to 5-cm) tube lures.

XTREME FACT – *Jigging the bait—moving it left, right, up, or down in a dancing motion—may make perch strike.*

Crappies

Crappies are tasty panfish that range in size from 9 to 10 inches (23 to 25 cm) and ½ to 1 pound (.23 to .45 kg). They bite during the first several hours of night and low-light morning time. However, a thick ice covering may make them active during the day.

XTREME FACT – The Crappie Flop Ice Fishing Tournament is held yearly at Lake Minnetonka in Excelsior, Minnesota. It raises money for local charities.

LAKE MINNETONKA ANNUAL ICE FISHING TOURNAMENT
CRAPPIE FLOP

Crappies "suspend" themselves in water. They do not hide at the bottom of lakes. Ice fishermen drop small bait or jigs down, but suspend their lures above the tops of weeds or just under the ice.

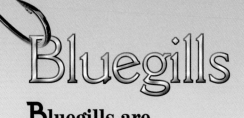

Bluegills

Bluegills are both feisty and delicious. They are popular ice fishing catches.

In winter, bluegills are found near the shallow parts of lakes, where there are lots of weeds. Although only about 5 to 8 inches (13 to 20 cm) long, they put up a good fight. They are school fish, so where there is one, there are often many.

XTREME FACT – Bluegills feed on small plankton, so anglers bait their lines with tiny jigs or small pieces of worms or mealworms.

Walleye

Walleye are big fish, ranging in length from 14 to 21 inches (36 to 53 cm). "Glass eyes" see well in dim light. Overcast winter days are a good time to catch them. Walleye are fighters usually found in deep water, or in shallower water where there is some protection, such as weeds. A strong fiberglass or graphite rod with large guides is needed. The large guides prevent freeze-ups as the wet line is reeled in.

XTREME FACT – Ice fishermen sometimes use bottom skipping to attract walleye. This jigging style allows the lure to drop down into the mud at the bottom. This stirs up silt and makes it look like the lure is feeding, thus attracting large predators such as walleye.

Northern Pike

The mighty northern pike is a toothy catch that's active in winter. Vibrations such as drilling holes or walking on ice may cause the wary fish to drop down to the weedy bottoms of lakes. Ice fishermen drill holes and drop their lines in these areas.

XTREME FACT – Northern pike have big "Y-bones" that must be eaten around. It is difficult to get rid of them when cleaning the fish.

Ice fishermen jig using baitfish or medium- or large-sized lures to attract northerns. Be prepared for a fight. These fish grow as big as 10 to 20 pounds (4.5 to 9 kg). Landing a northern is exciting!

Muskellunge

Muskellunge, commonly called "muskies," are a rare and exciting catch for ice fishermen. These trophy fish grow big, reaching 5 to 36 pounds (2 to 16 kg). Muskies or tiger muskies (a northern pike/muskie hybrid) are often an accidental catch when fishing for northerns. Muskies bite on big minnows, as well as jigging spoons and swimming lures. They often lurk near rocks or weeds.

Brook Trout

Brook trout are found in clear, pure lakes in the United States and Canada. Tip-ups are set with medium-sized minnows and jig lures. Brookies range in size from .6 to 6 pounds (.3 to 3 kg). They are a delicious fish.

Lake Trout

Lake trout love cold water. They are a popular catch with ice fishermen, as lakers will move up to snatch the angler's waiting bait.

Lake trout range in size from 2 to 4 pounds (.9 to 1.8 kg), but may reach up to 20 pounds (9 kg) or more. These are tasty fish often found in the Great Lakes area. It is important for anglers to stay quiet in order to attract and catch lake trout. These cautious fish spook easily.

Dangers

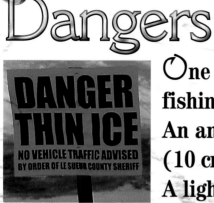

One of the great dangers of ice fishing is falling through thin ice. An angler needs at least 4 inches (10 cm) of ice to support his weight. A light truck needs 7.5 inches (19 cm) of ice. Warning signs of "thin ice" are often posted, but a person needs to be careful at all times. If there is broken or mottled gray ice near the shoreline, stay off. Chisels are often used to test the ice thickness every few steps. If the ice breaks, anglers must carefully back off the way they came.

XTREME FACT – The "pick of life" is a lifesaving device with points on either end of a short rope. Ice fishermen carry this safety device to help pull themselves out of the water if they fall through the ice.

Glossary

Auger

In ice fishing, a device used to drill holes in the ice. An auger may be powered by hand, gas, electricity, or propane.

Bob House

A New Hampshire name for an ice house. The name may have arisen because ice houses were brought onto the ice on bobsleds. Or it may be because the houses are short, or "bobbed." Or it may be because if an ice house is left on the lake too long, it will be "bobbing" in water.

Chisel

A long-handled stick-like device with a sharpened end used by ice fishermen to cut holes in ice.

Fiberglass

A reinforced plastic material, fiberglass is made of glass fibers embedded in a resin. Fishing rods made of fiberglass are flexible and tough, but may be heavier than rods made of other materials, such as graphite.

Graphite

A material used to make lighter-yet-stronger, more-sensitive fishing rods.

Jig Pole

A 2- to 3-foot (.6 to .9 m) -long fiberglass pole. The reel is very basic. It is only used to hold the fishing line, since there is no casting in ice fishing. Anglers "jig," or jerk the rod up and down or left and right, to attract fish.

Jiggle Stick

An ice fishing pole without a reel. The stick is often made of wood with the fishing line attached. The angler drops the line and bait in the water and jiggles it up and down or left and right to attract a fish's attention. If the bait is taken, the angler pulls the line up by hand.

Panfish

Smaller fish, such as perch or crappies, that easily fit in a skillet or pan.

Plankton

Tiny or microscopic organisms that float or drift in huge numbers in both freshwater and saltwater. Bluegills feed on plankton.

Predator

An animal or fish that feeds on other animals or fish.

School Fish

Fish of the same type and size that swim together.

Index